Opportunity Seized, Squandered, Lost: An AI Business Parable

Mark Dallmeier and Edward Vasko

Published by s3ntry corp, 2024.

While every precaution has been taken in the preparation of this book, the publisher assumes no responsibility for errors or omissions, or for damages resulting from the use of the information contained herein.

OPPORTUNITY SEIZED, SQUANDERED, LOST: AN AI BUSINESS PARABLE

First edition. July 1, 2024.

Copyright © 2024 Mark Dallmeier and Edward Vasko.

ISBN: 979-8227268464

Written by Mark Dallmeier and Edward Vasko.

Table of Contents

OPPORTUNITY SEIZED, SQUANDERED, LOST:

AN AI BUSINESS PARABLE

By

Mark Dallmeier & Edward Vasko

Table of Contents

Prologue

First, a big thank you for engaging and participating in the journeys and conversations of the characters within the book. Our intent was to create relatable executive and employee characters and put them into real-world business scenarios that would inspire you to reflect and guide you in deciding how you will move forward with your own journey. We hope the concepts and situations captured within these stories can be used as a guide that will help you formulate and implement a personalized plan leveraging the latest "game-changing" and disruptive technology, called artificial intelligence (AI). For purposes of our engagement with you, we're talking specifically about large language models, or LLMs. We hope to show how businesses can forge a thoughtful path towards the successful implementation and utilization of AI, one that creates positive business outcomes, and sustainable business value.

Since its first public release in October 2022, Generative AI end user adoption has broken all previous technology adoption records. Within the first 18 months of its release, Generative AI technologies have captured a significant percentage of global media attention, diverted billions of dollars in venture capital and private equity investments to AI focused companies, and have driven hundreds of thousands of companies globally to begin testing AI within various areas of the business.

Due to the global AI mania that has been created by the media, and the billions of dollars being diverted into AI companies within the financial markets, AI is now top of mind for nearly every business leader and board member.

"How do we drive value from AI investments?" is often the question posed to executives from the board.

"If we don't utilize AI, our competition will!" is a statement of fear that often accompanies the first question.

This fear of being left behind or giving up a competitive advantage the company has in the market could be reason enough for some executive teams to drop other priorities and dive headfirst into the AI mania.

Yet, as with all seismic shifts in business and technology sectors—such as the release of the personal computer, the rise of the internet and the dot.com era, and the consumerization of applications now ubiquitous on tablets & smartphones—oftentimes, those who ride the first wave of these new technologies and business models are picked up in the wave and smashed against the rocks. This leaves the real opportunity for value creation to those who are thoughtful, have learned from history, and who plan and then execute a well-conceived and tested strategy. We hope you find this approach as useful as our characters within found it.

Finally, no forward would be complete without some "of the times" business statistics— what else allows us to drive multiple editions through the years? Tongue in cheek aside, a few statistics that stand out to us include:

- By 2026, GenAI will drive 35 percent of revenue generated by AI service providers, up from less than two percent in 2023.

- By 2027, more than half of the GenAI models used by enterprises will be domain-specific (industry or business function), up from one percent today.

- By 2028, the adoption of AI services specifically designed for sustainable business will grow to 20 percent, up from less than five percent today.

AI Planning Assumptions — Gartner April, 2024

About the Team

Mark Dallmeier and Ed Vasko have worked together for over a decade, delivering services and solutions to organizations within dozens of industries, globally. With (too many) decades of technology and executive leadership experience, this team has firsthand knowledge on how seismic, evolutionary shifts in technology can be leveraged by organizations to create value. These shifts can cause corporate and employee "extinction events," as they like to call them, if not handled properly and with the right mindset, causing more harm than good.

The scenarios and characters depicted within are entirely fictional and intended to help your organization become stronger, more resilient, and ultimately more successful than your competition, as you drive forward with your AI journey.

INTRODUCTION:
The AI Opportunity

Wellness Widgets: Opportunity Seized

Cheryl Blanchard hadn't felt this energized or excited about her work in nearly two decades.

Wellness Widgets, Inc.'s CEO left the *AI: Applications and Innovations* conference brimming with ideas. Her notebook was full of hastily scribbled notes outlining ways to implement the new technology.

She walked faster than usual across the packed parking lot to her car. Cheryl envisioned a more efficient company that brought more value to its customers *and* workers. That increased cash flow likely the outcome of this was, of course, also at the forefront of her mind. After all, that would ultimately be the fertile ground for Wellness Widgets to expand, but that wasn't what lay behind Cheryl's enthusiasm.

Cheryl had been in tech long enough to know that large language models, or LLMs, weren't anything new. She relied heavily on her spell checker and a grammar application to draft memos, reports, and emails. Both programs had a rudimentary understanding of context.

Wellness Widgets already used automated chatbots to process customer inquiries and perform several other functions. But Cheryl had a finely honed instinct for differentiating between technology that would genuinely change how people lived, worked, and played and hype-cycle tech.

Wellness Widgets wasn't her first startup, after all. But it also wasn't a startup anymore, precisely because Cheryl had successfully shepherded the company from its stereotypical studio-office beginnings to a company that now sold wellness apps, products, and personal coaching programs to people worldwide.

Despite her excitement, Cheryl forced herself to calm down. She had already quickly checked the time on her phone to see if it was too late to call her operations manager, Jack. Jack was going to be essential to the successful integration of AI. Cheryl knew that. He was particularly adept at turning abstract ideas into concrete, tangible processes. He'd also help her to determine who in the company would be necessary—and, hopefully, enthusiastic—about the AI integration and who may be more resistant to it.

Like anything new and potentially powerful, integrating AI into the company would have to be measured, exceptionally well thought out, and carefully executed. The timelines would be long, relatively speaking, but would also need to be adaptable to the quickly evolving technology.

There was a lot to consider in relation to technology as well. Cheryl thought back to conversations she had overheard as she walked the office. Some of her reports were terrified of generative AI. They thought it was coming for their jobs. But Cheryl envisioned an opportunity for more internal promotions.

She had other concerns, too. One panel at the conference centered on copyright concerns had particularly struck her as a warning bell. Then, of course, there was privacy, proprietary data, inadvertent plagiarism, and hallucinations to consider as well. It would be all too easy for a misleading or inaccurate description of one of their supplements to land Wellness Widgets in court. Here again, Cheryl saw an opportunity to elevate existing employees while increasing process efficiencies.

That was the most exciting part for Cheryl. She was eager to explore how AI could be integrated into some Wellness Widgets operations to create more internal value. If her employees could get questions answered more quickly while simultaneously reducing grunt work, Cheryl was certain the department would ultimately become more productive and creative.

Cheryl climbed into her car and cued up her favorite podcasts for the three-hour drive back to the office. She reflected that she was glad she had spent the money and time to attend the conference. It had been a good investment. Both the customers and employees of Wellness Widgets were about to get much more satisfaction from the company.

SoftAware: Opportunity Squandered

Mike Stanfordson stepped out of the San Diego hotel's conference center lobby.

He was the CEO of a successful wellness company that had grown from small beginnings into a well-known national name brand. SoftAware employed over seven hundred people and had three office locations strategically spread across the country on the East Coast, in the Midwest, and its original home office in Silicon Valley.

SoftAware had leveraged a small, moderately successful gym equipment line into a fitness movement with something of a cult following. Their branding was licensed to gym franchises that used SoftAware gym machines and employed personal fitness coaches who taught SoftAware's comprehensive fitness and nutrition regimens. Many of these gyms sold SoftAware's nutritional supplements, drinks, and other fitness accessories, such as sophisticated smartwatches and headphones.

The company's clients also included governmental and private organizations that operated at a national, and not infrequently international, level. They built SoftAware gyms in their office buildings, and employees received premium access to SoftAware's fitness apps.

To Mike, SoftAware could only get bigger, and he saw AI as the perfect way to accelerate his plans. In his mind, Mike had already slashed operating costs by thirty percent. His list of ways to implement AI was pages long before the first day of the conference had ended.

The company could also eliminate the copywriting department and most of the marketing reps, keeping one or two people on as editors. Mike acknowledged that hallucinations were a point of concern. But he was confident that within a few years, generative AI would be advanced enough that hallucinations would be a thing of the past. And besides, Mike thought, that's what the lawyers were for.

Mike quickly ran through several tasks that would no longer need a human to complete—departmental reports, obviously, market projections, repetitive internal and external orders, marketing campaigns, and order processing (already mostly automated). He was positively giddy thinking about the number of meetings that could be eliminated now.

For years, Mike had chafed at what he felt were the unnecessary inefficiencies and lack of automation in the company, if not the industry as a whole. Generative AI seemed to offer a tantalizing new future in which countless irritants that slowed growth would finally be eliminated. In his heart, he already believed this to be true.

Mike wasn't as worried about data storage or privacy concerns, even though he had attended the same information security panel as Cheryl. First, his company had a robust legal team. He made a mental note to add vendor contract review and compliance checking to his AI implementation list since their proprietary software dealt with sensitive information. Second, he could train the employees to enter prompts into the AI software that did not include proprietary information. For Mike, who was definitely a businessman, not a technologist, this was an eminently solvable problem.

He didn't have a formal plan, so much as an intention to review SoftAware's processes, tools, and people and plug generative AI or LLM-based tools into those slots. Mike saw no reason the user-friendly tech couldn't be fully integrated within a few months.

In fact, as far as Mike was concerned, the list of problems solvable by AI was practically never-ending. He had already emailed his director of operations, marketing director, and chief financial officer links to one of the generative AI models briefly demonstrated during one of the conference's panels. Mike instructed them to spend some time getting familiar with it and to be prepared to discuss a rapid onboarding of the new, omnipresent AI "employee" on Monday.

Mike's enthusiasm had a tinge of righteousness, too. After all, he'd been asking for this technology for ten years. He cheerfully greeted the ride-share driver who pulled up to the conference center. Mike smiled to himself the whole way back to his hotel.

TechEeez: Opportunity Lost

Lisa Sutherland wasn't at the generative AI conference.

As founder and CEO of TechEeez, Lisa had to keep herself from rolling her eyes when the flashy email with an "exclusive" invitation for "tech and industry leaders" dinged into her inbox. As far as Lisa was concerned, all the hype over AI was equivalent to the panic over Y2K or, worse yet, the dizzying gold rush for cryptocurrency. While not non-existent, Lisa simply didn't believe generative AI merited all the enthusiasm for it.

Lisa wasn't opposed to new technology, but she had been in this game long enough to know it was, as of yet, essentially unproven. She could appreciate some of the grunt work AI would eliminate, but she couldn't envision it having that large of an impact on TechEeez's cash flow. A pragmatist at heart, the more excited people were about generative AI, the more Lisa tended to see its adoption as an emotional decision. She had heard and read very little about increased valuations for early adopter companies. That meant learning about generative AI wasn't worth investing the cost of a plane ticket, hotel, or valuable time that she could spend overseeing the company.

After all, Lisa had fought long and hard to turn TechEeez into a profitable company with positive cash flow. The success of her small, 230-employee, one-office company was based on a slow and steady growth strategy Lisa believed had served TechEeez well. She didn't move fast and break things, and while she wanted the company to grow, she also did not aspire to turn the organization into a tech company behemoth.

Still, Lisa had a vision for TechEeez, too. For the past four years, she had been slowly putting the pieces in place to prepare the company to expand from software used by coaches for elite athletes and sports franchises into the fitness hardware sector. She didn't necessarily want to become the next SoftAware, but she wanted to be successful enough to make them nervous.

OPPORTUNITY SEIZED, SQUANDERED, LOST: AN AI BUSINESS PARABLE

Lisa was especially proud of her small but mighty tech team, each member of which she'd personally recruited. Lisa didn't believe generative AI so easily supplanted their talent, and if not adopting the technology meant they innovated a bit slower, then so be it. TechEeez had a solid customer base, and Lisa wanted to focus more on customer and employee retention rather than endless, relentless, costly growth in any case.

Lisa deleted the email invitation and moved on to the next in her never-ending inbox. As she drafted a response to one of her sales reps, her AI grammar assistant alerted her to a few typos. Writing and grammar were never among Lisa's strengths, and she tended to hurry through emails anyway.

She reviewed a report from her finance director with suggestions on updating some T&E policies and methodically worked her way through the emails in her priority inbox. Other emails, like industry newsletters or group correspondence, were automatically filtered into different folders by her email client. When she encountered a large, complex contract that a prospective client's legal team had redlined, she sighed and decided she would need more coffee to slog through it. Remembering a new coffee shop in the area, she cued up her phone's map app and got directions.

As Lisa packed up her bag and mentally prepared for the tasks ahead of her, it never once occurred to her that in the last hour, she'd already used several iterations of AI to get work done. From the automatic filtering of her emails and grammar checker to the directions that would automatically reroute if she came across traffic or construction, the next iteration of AI that Lisa had so easily dismissed was already woven into the fabric of her business and daily life. She didn't realize she hadn't cleverly avoided a fad so much as to opt out of a powerful next evolution in business and technology.

Lisa had no idea how much this lack of curiosity about generative AI would impact her company over the next few months, but she would find out soon enough.

CHAPTER 1:
Implementing AI

Wellness Widgets: Easy Does It

Cheryl scanned the faces stretching down the long conference table staring back at her. What she saw did not surprise her. Just about every emotion imaginable was reflected back at her, from obvious worry to barely constrained enthusiasm.

Joan, her marketing director, looked absolutely terrified. This was despite Cheryl's numerous assurances that the goal was not to replace whole teams within the company but rather to strengthen their capabilities. Despite this, Joan's expression hadn't changed during the meeting.

This worried Cheryl, who had a fairly close work friendship with Joan and knew the marketing director pretty well. She had expected some hesitancy on Joan's part, maybe concern, but it was clear Joan was well beyond worried. Mentally, Cheryl made a note to set aside some time to think of ways to ease the implementation on Joan and other employees like her. Cheryl knew Joan would not be the only one who heard this announcement as bad news.

Meanwhile, Jack, the director of operations who frequently also played the role of product lead, looked worried, too, but also determined. He'd reacted just as Cheryl had predicted he would. Seeing the change management challenges ahead, Jack's legal pad was covered with notes. He'd peppered Cheryl with questions throughout the meeting and was by far the most prepared and vocal of the group.

Several of the department leads—Alan, the CFO; Marcia, the HR generalist; and Tammy, the CTO—looked pleased and excited.

Morgan, who led the customer service and consumer outreach divisions, remained a mystery to Cheryl. During her presentation, Cheryl made it clear that Morgan's department would likely be the most impacted by the organizational implementation of generative AI. Morgan didn't appear opposed to the idea, but he didn't seem enthused, either.

Then there were Jessica and Todd, the attorneys Wellness Widgets had used for years. They came from an external, well-respected corporate law firm that specialized in tech law, specifically IP matters. Cheryl knew they'd play a huge role in the company-wide implementation and had asked them to sit in on the meeting. Both attorneys looked concerned. Still, Cheryl suspected the law firm would ultimately be happy to have a real test client for the new tech.

After letting the silence from the last round of questions settle, Cheryl decided a bit more reassurance was in order.

"I'm going to say it again because it's worth repeating," she said, making it a point to make eye contact with everyone briefly. "This is an opportunity we can't afford to miss, but we're not going to barrel into it with our eyes closed."

"But how can our eyes be open when there's so much we still don't know?" asked Morgan. "It's totally new technology. I've read in the news it makes some pretty serious mistakes, too. If you think the damage a bad review can do is bad, imagine a customer getting the wrong guidance or mistakenly denied a refund or new device."

Cheryl saw the legal heads nod and Joan's brow furrow even more.

"That's why we're going to test every implementation in-house first," Cheryl said. "Nothing is going to be launched until everyone who uses this technology—and our legal team— is satisfied it's ready."

"This is really fast-moving tech, though," Tammy said. "My team and I have been spending a lot of time just trying to keep up with the latest versions and developments. And that's just knowing about it, not even using it! AI may not be new, but the evolution of generative AI platforms is—three versions in months! *Mere months!*"

Cheryl tried not to let her mild impatience show.

"That's why you're such a crucial part of this, Tammy, and I know you're up to the challenge," she said. "As long as you stay abreast of key developments relevant to this organization's specific, *targeted* integration of AI, I'm confident we'll be fine."

Cheryl glanced at the clock on her laptop. The meeting had gone half an hour over the scheduled time, but she didn't mind because, as she'd expected, there had been a lot of questions. Some focused on what she had shared from the AI conference, while others focused more on how generative AI would specifically be used at Wellness Widgets.

Cheryl didn't always have the answers to the questions, and she knew that made some of her reports very uncomfortable. But she also hadn't gotten this company to its longest profitability streak in five years by being inflexible. Cheryl trusted in the established but open process she'd put in place. Questions were an opportunity for more data, and she was grateful for them.

Each of the direct reports was asked to develop a survey with their respective department managers to identify workflow pain points. Since Cheryl had been meaning to do a job satisfaction survey anyway, it was a good opportunity to kill two birds with one stone. A static survey wouldn't work in this situation, Cheryl knew, because of the way generative AI could be used in a variety of forms. While marketing may want to use it to generate text and images, the IT department may be more interested in an interactive troubleshooting chatbot. The finance department may prefer to use it solely for analysis summaries.

They were charting new waters, and that meant letting information lead the way. Cheryl found this to be one of the most exciting parts of being an executive, but she knew uncertainty made others in the organization uncomfortable.

In two weeks, Cheryl and her direct reports would go over the survey and identify specific pain points that generative AI could address. Then, she would work closely with Tammy and her team to assess how feasible implementing AI in that area would be, practically speaking.

For the most part, Cheryl left optimistic. Whatever qualms he may have, it was clear Jack was on board and that, she knew, was going to be a huge part of this initiative's success. She was a bit disappointed with Morgan's reaction but trusted him to at least give generative AI a fair shot. And, since the customer service department had the most generative AI adaptable tasks, Cheryl was reasonably confident Morgan would be on board soon enough. Morgan was generally well liked by his entire department, so Cheryl appreciated how important having Morgan's buy-in would be.

Then there was Tammy. Equal to, if not more important than, Jack, her initial reaction had surprised Cheryl a bit. Tammy loved new tech, so Cheryl wasn't the least bit surprised when she mentioned that her team had been following generative AI developments closely. What Cheryl hadn't expected was the level of fear and worry Tammy had shown during the meeting.

Still, Tammy was a passionate woman who could sometimes come off as overly strident, so Cheryl decided to wait a bit before determining where Tammy stood. Cheryl also knew Tammy was more than capable of spearheading this, but she wasn't sure *Tammy* knew that about herself. Cheryl made a mental note to have a one-on-one with Tammy to explain why she was willing to put this crucial company evolution largely in Tammy's hands. Maybe this would be an excellent growth opportunity for Tammy.

Cheryl tried to ignore a heavy knot of worry in the bottom of her stomach that formed when she glanced over at Joan, who was morosely staring at her locked laptop screen. Internally, Cheryl sighed. It was going to take a bit of extra work to get Joan fully invested in this change, but she had yet to lose hope that Joan would be standing with her once they fully launched generative AI. It was a personal concern for Cheryl, too, as she genuinely valued their friendship.

The legal team would also be heavily involved at this stage, primarily to ensure that any software used or designed in-house wasn't a liability nightmare. Cheryl also instinctually sensed that Wellness Widgets needed to disclose to some degree how AI was being used while maintaining proprietary standards.

The departments and teams would test the new technology internally for several weeks. As employees adapted to making generative AI part of their workflow, they would offer feedback to Tammy's IT team. Cheryl had already authorized

Tammy to either promote specific people from her department for this task or hire new members, effectively creating a dedicated IT sub-team to handle AI.

Cheryl, worried, glanced at Joan again. Joan looked miserable and was silently tracing the outline of her keyboard keys with a finger. Cheryl made a note to have a one-on-one with Joan the very next day. Joan was very good at her job, and Cheryl had reached a bit financially to meet Joan's salary demands. The past five years had proven it to be a good investment, but Cheryl understood having everyone on board was crucial for implementation to be successful.

Pushback was one thing, but adopting generative AI was not optional. Cheryl felt deeply certain about that and hoped that Joan was not a flight risk. After all, she had invested heavily in Joan and her department and would not want to retrain another leader for that department. Especially in the midst of such a huge sea change for the company.

SoftAware LLC: Full Steam Ahead

"So, what are we looking at in terms of a timeline?" Mike asked Dominique, the CTO of SoftAware, LLC.

"Well, I mean, there's still a lot here to consider," Dominique said. "We have to decide what we're doing in-house. And for that, I'll need a full-stack developer, at least."

Dominique paused when he saw Mike's eyes harden a bit. Mike, Dominique knew, was a numbers guy who ran—quite successfully—a very lean organization. Dominique had always appreciated that Mike knew the tech team was not the most efficient place to cut corners. But his boss and longtime friend's excitement about generative AI was concerning him for a number of reasons.

"It's just that it's not as simple as the news and everyone makes it sound," Dominique said. "There's still a lot we don't know about how applying this tech will turn out. And there's some pretty serious security concerns, too."

Mike barely contained his frustrated sigh. He tapped two fingers on his desk.

"OK," he said. "Here's what I need from you."

Dominique felt his stomach clench but didn't reply.

"Get me a list of software or apps we can start deploying next week in customer service, marketing, and any of our online self-service platforms. I'm holding on to our marketing director for now; we need them to check the generative content and guide any accelerated automated processes. We'll keep a few copywriters for editing, but we'll be reducing that department significantly. And let's figure out how to level up our chatbot, too."

"That's way easier said than done," Dominique said. "Our chatbot *is* automated. It's already a basic version of AI, but we had to tweak it to include customer-specific requests. The same goes for the marketing emails; that's already automated, but it's still guided automation."

"Great, so this won't take long at all!" Mike grinned.

"Right, but *we* developed our chatbot with *the* proprietary information used to develop *our* products," Dominique tried to explain. "If we just upload our information and chat catalog into another platform, that software company will have access to all our information. And we can't guarantee it'll be secure because it's on their servers. Plus, we don't know how that company will use our info for its learning models."

"That's why we have a compliance department, to read user license agreements, though, right?"

"Well, I mean, yeah," Dominique said. "But our customers still trust us to at least attempt to prevent data breaches. And I'm just not sure that integrating another platform without checking with our vendors and subs is honoring that trust. Or their EULAs, come to think of it."

He stopped when he saw how much Mike's face had darkened.

"Look, I'm really excited about this, too," Dominique said. "And I agree with you that this is going to be huge for us. We should absolutely be at the front of this wave. I'm just saying it's not quite as set-it-and-forget-it as this conference may have led you to believe."

Mike started to get up from the desk and pack his laptop in his bag, signaling the meeting was essentially over. This rankled Dominique, but he bit his tongue, more in service to the close friendship the two men had developed over the past several years than anything else.

"Look, whatever you need to get this done, and as quickly as possible, consider it granted," Mike said. "This tech is moving so fast that I'm sure there's already updated, new versions we can leverage that have been created in just a couple of days since I got back."

Dominique nodded. On that, at least, they agreed.

"OK, I'll have something in your inbox in a few days," Dominique said, getting up to leave.

But he wasn't as excited as he had initially been when he saw the invitation to meet to discuss AI. In fact, now he was just worried.

Dominique knew there was an incredible opportunity here to make history. Done correctly, SoftAware could create cutting-edge generative AI platforms with technology that might be adaptable to other industries. There was a lot to learn, and the technology was being adopted and accelerating faster than anything he'd seen before. And Dominique saw generative AI as a thrilling challenge.

Though he'd been at SoftAware for most of his career, Dominique had a reputation for being creative and for quickly innovating adaptable enterprise systems. He frequently presented at highly technical conferences and had turned down some impressive and occasionally more lucrative research and development opportunities.

But he and Mike had been friends for a very long time and had built SoftAware together. The company felt as much like his as Mike's. Mike had given Dominique a lot of room to take risks, try new things, and occasionally disrupt the health and fitness tech space. What outsiders mistook as career complacency was really Dominique making a strategic choice in the name of personal and professional exploration. He understood just how beneficial it was to have a CEO who would go to bat for him at shareholder meetings, and that he had leeway with Mike he would not have in most other companies of this size.

Finally, there was his team. Mostly younger guys, Dominique took their careers as seriously as his own. He was known for investing a lot of time in his team, always encouraging them to expand their skill sets. Much to his very understanding wife's exasperation, it wasn't uncommon for Dominique to spend long evenings after work talking with or mentoring some of the junior developers and new software engineers.

In both his field and his company, Dominique was a servant leader who was personally invested in innovation. On some level, he knew Mike didn't fully understand that—Mike was a business guy through and through—but Dominique didn't need Mike to understand that.

Until now. For the first time, Dominique felt truly opposed to Mike's thinking, vision, and direction. But he also knew he was in the best position to protect SoftAware from Mike's impatience, technical ignorance, and sometimes monomaniacal focus on cash flow and growth.

So, that was exactly what Dominique would do.

TechEeez: Toe in the Water

Lisa looked up at the knock on her door to see Kristy, her CFO, standing in the doorway clutching a very thick sheaf of papers.

"Hey boss, you have a sec?" Kristy asked.

"Sure," Lisa said. In truth, she was immersed in end-of-quarter reports and trying to prepare to mentally run the tax season gauntlet. But she took her open-door policy very seriously and so mentally set aside what she was looking at.

Kristy took a seat across from Lisa's desk.

"I was just reading up on how this new generative AI is being used in different companies and departments," Kristy began. "And I think it would be hugely helpful to my team, particularly in cutting down how long it takes us to get our analysis reports to you."

Lisa sighed internally. She, too, had been reading up on the various iterations the "new" tech was taking in different businesses. The mistakes—hallucinations, erroneous advice given to users, copyright questions—were enough to make her stop reading most of the articles that were increasingly cluttering her inbox.

"We're not behind on anything that I know of," Lisa said, being careful not to say no or dismiss Kristy out of hand. She wanted her employees to know they could talk to her and she'd take them seriously.

But she was also getting exasperated and frustrated with what she saw as a fad technology. She had lived through zeitgeists before. The last one even cost her a company. Lisa was not about to throw her carefully crafted stability and growth foundation away on the basis of what, from the little she did read about it, was essentially spicy autocomplete.

"Well, no, not really," Kristy agreed. "But the thing is, that's a huge part of our overall product acquisition and development process. So, if we could cut those hours, and sometimes even days, down to less than a fraction of the time, then we could potentially increase our offerings and on a much shorter timeline."

Lisa didn't say anything, so Kristy went on.

"I mean, this could help us break into hardware even faster—"

"Until it makes a far more serious, more easily overlooked computer error," Lisa said. "I'm sure you're also familiar with its hallucinations?"

Kristy's face fell.

"But go on, make your case," Lisa said, regretting how terse she sounded but still always willing to debate.

"Well, we'd still have to review the reports for accuracy," Kristy said. "I'm not suggesting a totally hands-off approach. But every time we ran a report, it would get better because it's learning from us. At least, that's what I understand from talking to Andrew."

Andrew was TechEeez's CTO. He'd worked his way up from a junior position and was one of the company's oldest employees. Lisa never lost sight of the fact that much of the company's success was squarely due to Andrew's skill and good judgment.

"What did Andrew have to say about it?" Lisa asked, genuinely curious. She hadn't brought anything to Andrew because she didn't want to waste his time.

"Well, he agrees with me, basically," Kristy said. "Actually, he said he's going to talk to you about how we can add generative AI into several of our departments, including his."

Slightly annoyed that her reports were having these conversations without her and not *with* her, Lisa remained determined to hear Kristy out. She would certainly at least listen to what Andrew had to say. And, to be fair, she *had* made passing comments dismissing generative AI as a tech hype cycle in meetings.

Still, Lisa was the CEO and founder of a tech company, so she could hardly dismiss AI out of hand. Especially if her employees were this curious about it. Hype or not, Lisa understood she had to learn more about it at least.

"OK, how about this?" Lisa asked. "Let's get you, me, Andrew, and a couple of other department heads in a room next week and discuss this."

"Well, that seems like a long time," Kristy said, visibly excited. "Andrew said we have to adopt this quick—"

"I'm sure we can catch up with four days of development," Lisa said, trying to keep the sarcasm from her voice. "And I'm more concerned about the IRS deadlines at the moment."

She softened this last bit with a smile, but Kristy's crestfallen expression remained.

"Yeah, well, OK," Kristy said, standing up. "But you know, a lot of auditors are adopting generative AI, too, and that's really valuable for us on the CFO side. So, really, if you want to embed generative AI into our annual—"

"I think that's a perfect topic to bring up during the meeting," Lisa said.

Lisa's dismissiveness stung Kristy a bit, but she was grateful there would at least be a meeting about it. Still, as she walked back to her office, Kristy couldn't help but feel a prickly sense of frustration bubble up in her chest.

How was Lisa expecting to keep the company relevant to its customers if, as a trusted fitness tech company, it wasn't using AI? Or even testing it, for that matter. The company's customer base included the world's most elite athletes, their trainers, and global sports franchises. By their very nature, customers were constantly looking for the next thing that could give them a competitive edge, and Kristy knew they would be the first to adopt AI-powered fitness technology.

TechEeez had a reputation—no, an obligation, really—to be at the forefront of innovations like this one. After all, if generative AI could help a future Olympiad win a gold medal, shouldn't TechEeez be a part of that journey? She was no marketing expert, but she knew their logo in stadiums and on athletic jerseys hadn't hurt the brand, even if it wasn't the largest logo there.

But then doubt started to nibble at Kristy's frustration. She remembered Lisa was the CEO and founder and trusted that Lisa knew what was best for the company. However, the truth was that trust was beginning to erode.

She left. Lisa made a note to schedule the promised meeting and returned her reports.

CHAPTER 2:
The Race is On

<u>Wellness Widgets: Moving Fast *Without* Breaking Things</u>

Joan, the marketing director at Wellness Widgets, nervously fidgeted with the edge of her portfolio as she waited outside Cheryl's office. She'd barely been able to eat or sleep since the meeting announcing the AI initiative almost two months ago.

Everywhere Joan turned, people were excitedly talking about generative AI and what it could do. Which was everything she and her team did.

It boggled Joan's mind how people could ask her if she was excited about the changes coming. She already had to handle two crying employees in her office. First, there was the fraught meeting with an experienced copywriter, Marcia, followed by an equally difficult meeting with Joe, her lead graphic designer.

Marcia and Joe were smart, talented, and worked hard—and both were utterly convinced they were obsolete. Even worse, Joan felt the same way about *her* position. Sharing the fears and concerns of her direct reports made it very difficult for Joan to authentically reassure her team, whose section of the option seemed to have a palpable shroud of worry over it.

Still, Joan tried to tell concerned team members all the talking points she'd been told over and over again in her conversations with Cheryl. At this point, it felt almost like a script. She would sit down, try to look reassuring, and begin to discuss how even advanced AI models still needed human oversight and how the technology was still, ultimately, a software platform that needed people to enter prompts.

Some of her team silently accepted this, or at least pretended to do so, but Marcia and Joe did not.

"But I don't *want* to be a prompt engineer!" Marcia had exclaimed loud enough to make Joan wince. "I like the creative part of my job, thinking of new ways to tell people about our products. I don't *want* some machine doing that for me!"

"It isn't, not really," Joan had said, not sure she believed that herself. "Think of it like a coworker or an intern. You'll assign it a task and then review and alter its work as you see fit."

"*This* is not how I would talk to an intern," the copywriter said, anger creeping into her voice. She waved the prompt cheat sheet that had been emailed to her department that morning at Joan. "This is *data entry*! It's not writing, branding, or marketing; it is the *exact opposite* of creativity and..."

Marcia began sputtering. She pulled herself up in her chair and slammed the prompt sheet on Joan's desk. "I'm not sure this is going to be the right role for me anymore," she said, her voice wavering on the last word and blinking rapidly to keep the tears in her eyes from falling.

For a moment, Joan herself was at a loss, taken aback by the sudden turn of the conversation. In a flash of defensive anger, she imagined telling Marcia to just leave, but that immediately softened into worry, concern and, for some reason, guilt, as though *she* had made Marcia cry.

Joan was a good manager and took a lot of pride in the fact her team genuinely seemed to like her and working with her. The marketing department was known for its more casual vibe in the office, which was common for creative departments in corporate environments. Joan knew how to give her team the freedom and autonomy necessary for them to create new campaigns and ideas but still reign in some of the more laissez-faire tendencies of some of the department members.

However, she was not a counselor and felt totally unprepared to deal with an intensely emotional conversation like this in a work setting. Especially when she saw so many of her own concerns and fears reflected back at her from Marcia's now tear-streaked face. She grabbed a tissue from the cabinet behind her and walked out from behind her desk to sit next to Marcia in the other seat.

OPPORTUNITY SEIZED, SQUANDERED, LOST: AN AI BUSINESS PARABLE

Handing the tissue to Marcia, who took it while looking away, Joan softly said, "I know this is a lot of change and can feel overwhelming."

Marcia sniffed, obviously now embarrassed by her outburst. Joan pointedly continued as though it were a more normal conversation.

"We're all adjusting to, well, all of this," Joan continued. "But I promise you, if you're at this company, it's because we value your contribution."

"But I don't know what I'm contributing anymore," Marcia said. "Writing the prompts doesn't feel like creating. It feels like data entry. A prompt isn't the same as actually writing the product copy or case study. That's the part I *like* doing."

Joan sighed softly. She completely understood how Marcia felt and shared the sentiment, but she also had an obligation to the company that she still took very seriously. After all, the company's success had happened largely due to the marketing department she had essentially built from scratch. Marcia had been one of Joan's first recruits, in fact.

"Look, we're still figuring out how we're going to integrate all this," Joan said. "Maybe for you, or all the content writers, it's more an editor than an actual writer. Maybe we can just use it to do all that annoying math."

Marcia smiled at the joke, much to Joan's relief.

"And let's face it, email nurturing campaigns are tedious. That's a perfect generative AI job, right?" she continued.

Marcia furrowed her brow and paused for a moment.

"Yeah, I mean, I guess," she said.

"Nothing is set in stone yet about how we're going to use this," Joan said, gently patting Marcia's arm.

Letting her voice harden just a bit, Joan waited a bit before continuing.

"However, trusting in the process and giving this time, the ability to be flexible and adapt, *is* a key qualification of this position."

Marcia immediately looked like she was on the verge of tears again, and Joan felt like she had just kicked a whimpering puppy.

"So what?" Marcia retorted, her voice cracking. "Twenty-three years of experience, keeping up with changing trends, going to trainings and conferences, spending my free time networking, spending mornings reading about analytics and methodologies, is just...nothing? Just like that, I'm replaced by a robot?"

Joan turned a deep sigh into a quiet, long exhale and tried to offer a reassuring smile.

"We wouldn't be having this conversation if that were the case," Joan said. "I won't lie. Your job—mine, too, for that matter—is going to look very different. And yes, some of the more creative aspects may be diminished. But you're not being replaced, at least not if you can adapt, OK?"

Marcia looked down in her lap but didn't respond. After a while, she wiped her face, mumbled an apology, and abruptly got up, leaving Joan sitting in her empty office.

Joan had a hard time focusing that day. She felt emotionally exhausted and had an increasing and hardening sense of resentment, too. Her department was good and helped the company succeed, but it was beginning to feel like all the disruption and angst, not to mention training and educational time, was just fixing something that wasn't broken.

The conversation with Joe the next day wasn't much better. Since he was younger, Joan had assumed he would be fine with, if not excited about, the addition of generative AI.

Joe was fresh out of college, and Wellness Widgets was his first job since graduation. But Joe's fear when he sat down in front of Joan had changed the feeling of the entire room.

In fact, Joan hadn't been able to shake the memory of that fear in Joe's eyes. Equally haunting was the way his voice wavered when he explained he had taken out additional student loans to get an MFA in digital design concepts. Joe had added, rather pointedly, that advanced degrees were increasingly the minimum requirement to apply for his role, including the one at Wellness Widgets.

"I mean, I just proposed to my girlfriend, and she really wants kids," Joe had said. "We both have student loans. Like, how do I ever get promoted if the AI is learning from me how to do my job better?"

Joan had given Joe the same spiel about adaptability and change, which was met with a hard cynicism.

"Right, so I'm like the auto worker going to Mexico to train my replacement, right?" Joe had said, not even trying to hide the angry disgust from his voice. "And then when the generative AI is all trained up, I just get fired and have a useless degree and a 100K of debt. Cool."

Perhaps because of his youth, Joe had not bothered to keep the disdain and sarcasm from his voice. Tempted to make a sharp comment about professionalism, Joan once again restrained herself.

"Look, even I don't know exactly what this is going to look like for any of us," Joan said. "But I would ask that you keep in mind you have an extraordinary opportunity to be a part of this company's growth and evolution."

Joe had responded with a barely disguised eye roll.

"You may look back someday and laugh at how you feel right now," Joan added with a weak smile.

"Yeah, sure," Joe replied, getting up to leave. "Well, guess there's nothing else to say about it."

Joan, once again, was left shrouded in the heavy silence of her empty office.

Her irritation at Joe's borderline impertinence faded into bemusement. She remembered when she was that age, fresh out of school with a degree that today would be considered generalist. Twenty-four years ago, however, earning a degree that separated marketing from advertising, and with courses that differentiated between television and radio formats from print marketing materials was a novelty.

It suddenly struck Joan that she had once been exactly where Joe was. She had chosen to focus on graphic design and had been hired by a luxury fashion brand's marketing department. Joan remembered how the department had not one but *two* desktop PCs known for their graphical capabilities. She remembered being excited when she learned to use them—no more color separating and pre-pressing the settings by hand.

But why didn't she feel this way about generative AI? Joan wasn't opposed to tech, after all. It was why she was excited about the position at Wellness Widgets.

Yet she felt the same way as Marcia and Joe. It was one thing to drag and drop a magazine spread layout. That *was certainly* easier than cutting paper and sticking it to galleys with beeswax.

But in that case, she was still the *creator*. What photo to use, how much text, where it went, the colors, the pagination—all that came from *her*. With generative AI, all that came from her was a sentence typed into a box that said, "Create a magazine layout with this information in a style reminiscent of vintage *Vogue* but using HD-compatible saturation."

There is no choosing color, no ideating a vision, no playing with movement and feel, no intellectually leaping off a cliff of inspiration or choosing what parts to put together in a new way. Just...giving instructions.

Marcia's comment about being reduced to a data entry person came back to Joan, and her brow furrowed as it began to feel true.

But then she remembered why she had applied to Wellness Widgets six years ago. The company she was at, an advertising firm, was holding on to clients who produced products that Joan knew were destined to be outdated. She was excited by tech advancements and wanted the challenge of inspiring that excitement in the masses.

One of the first things she did when creating the marketing department was figure out a budget for the tech stack, or all the software, equipment, and devices she would need. She knew not everyone in her department used the tech available to them in the same way, with some relying on it more than others. Plenty of her reports took notes in a notebook and then generated digital campaigns.

Taking a deep breath, Joan swiveled her chair around and looked at the view outside her office. She was starting to feel better. If she could convince Cheryl to give her a bit more leeway in how and to what degree her department integrated generative AI, they could figure out a way to meet in the middle.

For her part, she decided to change the conversation from focusing on generative AI to reinforcing her team's capabilities and talents. That way, the new integrations wouldn't feel like they were subsuming her department's respective roles.

And then they would *all* get back to enjoying their work.

Cheryl hung up her phone after making an appointment with her legal firm and looked at the large, easel-style sheets of paper she'd hung on the wall across from her desk.

Progress was a bit slower than she would have liked, but things were undeniably moving forward.

After analyzing the employee surveys and meeting with all the departments, Cheryl began to implement what she believed was a decent AI integration strategy.

First, she mentally committed to taking a risk on vertical integration. That meant designing a platform specifically for Wellness Widgets, built primarily in-house. For efficiency's sake, it would be based on an existing framework offered by a local AI startup.

That solved several problems. It enabled the company to control what information, proprietary or public, was used and how. Most importantly, from the legal team's perspective, it enabled Wellness Widgets to control where data entered into the AI platform was stored and for how long. More than a technical issue, this decision enabled the company to better adapt to already changing compliance or regulations.

Each department would internally use the generative AI as it was developed and refined in-house. Customer service would augment its chatbots with real-time responses that incorporated the customer's history and analyzed their emotional tone. Specific issues would trigger an escalation to human assistance.

The customer service team was skeptical. Yet, only four days in, they seemed happier overall. Not having to deal with the lower, rote calls had freed up the more ambitious and driven representatives to develop or streamline new processes for some of the more complex issues that required more touchpoints. Though only hinted at in the surveys, Cheryl suspected the tedium of dealing with the simple, lower-tier calls was a rather large pain point that generative AI had eliminated. Which was exactly what Cheryl had hoped would happen.

It was a promising start to the internal test integration. Cheryl suspected there were similar pain points within other Wellness Widgets departments. She had even sent an email to all department heads encouraging them—and their teams—to be as honest as possible in the survey responses.

Even if it's not a problem, task, or process you believe generative AI can solve, I want to know about it, she had written. *This isn't just about us adopting new technology. It's about creating a stable company with high employee satisfaction so we are well positioned to reach the next growth cycle this new technology will take us to.*

After several back-and-forth conversations with department heads, Cheryl semi-reluctantly agreed to make survey results anonymous. The managers said this would increase participation and honesty, and they were right, too. Cheryl, unfamiliar with some of the more mechanical processes involved in the company, was a bit disappointed to learn there were quite so many pain points. That disappointment, however, was outweighed by her excitement that, in most cases, a custom generative AI platform could address those issues.

And, she remembered with a small smile that an unexpected and tangential benefit was closing some important salary compression gaps that had been uncovered. The addition of better coffee and new vending machine options in the break room were perks, too. Cheryl didn't mind the candy she occasionally tucked into her briefcase.

Still, some downsizing was unavoidable. The in-house development of a custom generative AI platform was costly, and ultimately, some of the new efficiencies resulted in redundancies. Wellness Widgets simply didn't need an entire room full of customer service representatives anymore. However, both Cheryl and Morgan had worked hard to either promote those who were ready for the challenge—and willing to embrace the GAI technology—or move them to a new department that needed a role filled.

Inevitably, people lost their jobs. However, Cheryl honestly felt that the number of layoffs had been kept as low as possible. More importantly, the dismissals were handled in an honest, ethical manner. She allowed her managers to give as much informal advance warning and lead time to redundant employees as legally possible. She encouraged all managers to offer references or referrals and made in-person meetings breaking the news mandatory. Morgan offered training or guidance to managers to help them learn to navigate the conversations.

Wellness Widgets would not end up on the front pages as another cold, heartless tech company throwing people into the wild.

Alan, the CFO, and his small team of three had wholeheartedly embraced the change. They were using an existing AI platform as a testing platform to extrapolate, consolidate, and analyze more data from longer time periods than had ever before been possible. They could get solid predictive analysis in hours with data that would have taken years to organize and collate in the first place. Then, they noted how they would improve upon the platform and sent those to Tammy and her team so the Wellness Widgets version would be nearly exactly aligned with the company's specific needs.

The ability to gather more complex analyses of data sets so remarkably quickly had already led to surprising results. Previously unidentified user trends were identified, revealing several new market opportunities. The accountants began to tentatively suggest Wellness Widgets could expand into hardware like custom gym equipment that adapted to a whole new suite of user metrics. As tantalizing an idea as that was, Cheryl gently told the team to wait until the full deployment was done before diving into that.

Using loose, hypothetical information, they went through mock workflows, taking note of any errors, issues, or repeated troubleshooting. Every week, without asking, Cheryl received an email from Alan with "suggestions" for the developers working on the in-house, custom GAI system, which she duly forwarded with comments to Tammy, her CTO.

Her meetings with Alan's team were, by far, Cheryl's favorite. The four accountants were energized and excited, but they often had to be slowed down and reminded they were still *testing* a platform to help develop Wellness Widgets' *beta* version. Still, Cheryl took the new energy in the finance corner as evidence of AI's positive impacts.

Tammy also had to be slowed down a bit. Cheryl had her hold off on using AI to assist in writing code for two new wearable products they planned to launch in a year, at least for now. For now, Tammy's team had to settle for using GAI to troubleshoot IT issues and write user-friendly self-help guides for internal use. Though Tammy chafed under the restrictions, she admitted it also created space for her team to focus on building the new platform.

The new IT manuals, created in minutes, significantly reduced the time the IT team spent resetting passwords and combing through spam emails. In addition to making the IT workers happy, almost everyone else liked the new system, too. It was easier than calling IT and waiting for someone. And, thanks to a careful but creative prompt, the manuals were also humorous and playful.

All of Cheryl's direct reports were held in near-continuous meetings with Jack, the director of operations. He flitted from department to department daily to ask questions, oversee processes, and sometimes even assist in training.

It all gave the company an all-hands-on-deck energy Cheryl hadn't felt since their startup days. Though she had moments of doubt—particularly when something went wrong, or the AI spat out nonsense or bad advice—overall, she was excited and invigorated by the past few weeks.

OPPORTUNITY SEIZED, SQUANDERED, LOST: AN AI BUSINESS PARABLE

The one dark cloud that seemed to linger over the office was Joan and the marketing team. The customer service layoffs did not help.

Cheryl and Joan were both ethically aligned with how Wellness Widgets handled the layoffs. Ever the professional marketer, Joan understood the importance of the public knowing everything Wellness Widgets did to soften the blow for employees who were laid off. Whatever other uncertainty Joan was grappling with, she still fiercely believed her primary job was to protect the Wellness Widgets brand. Cheryl was deeply grateful for Joan many times during the weeks that followed the initial round of layoffs. The company got through it without suffering damaging public derision.

Unfortunately, for Joan, it was like working on her worst nightmare in real time. She couldn't help but wonder if she'd soon be writing press releases and answering reporter inquiries about her department or even herself. Inevitably, the underlying tension began to fray the women's friendship.

Conversations the two women would normally have used as an excuse to chat in person or maybe grab a quick lunch together became short, overly efficient emails from Joan. They rarely stopped to chat when passing each other in the office or parking lot anymore, instead exchanging tight, wordless smiles before quickly breaking eye contact. The tone of any texts had become noticeably businesslike. Neither woman asked about personal developments in each other's lives anymore. Cheryl was left wondering whether Joan had gotten her mother into a specific nursing home, but she no longer felt comfortable asking Joan about it.

For her part, Cheryl wished she could vent to Joan about her challenges dealing with her recently retired husband, who had decided to turn their guest bedroom into a home beer distillery while Cheryl was on a work trip.

Now, it was emails and calendar invitations and as little in-person interaction as possible.

Joan was never rude, of course, and Cheryl was doing her best not to take the coldness and distance personally. Still, friendships with other driven women in their particular tech space were rare. For Cheryl, the time spent with Joan offered small but important bright spots that softened long and often grueling days.

There was no denying that the increased distance and coolness between the two women put a damper on Cheryl's focused enthusiasm for leading the company into this new chapter.

However, Cheryl also knew she needed a marketing director who was fully on board with the AI integration. And increasingly, she saw that simply wasn't the case with Joan.

While Joan did everything she was asked, Cheryl knew Joan wasn't convinced. Sometimes, Joan's questions seemed more about finding fault with the new processes than implementing the latest technology. Cheryl was increasingly frustrated but unsure how else she could accommodate Joan's fears.

As a last-ditch effort, she allowed Joan to integrate generative AI independently into her department, even allowing marketing to lag behind other areas in the company.

<u>SoftAware: Spaghetti at the Wall</u>

Dominique, the CTO of SoftAware, sighed and tapped his laptop trackpad. He stared at the screen and focused on clenching down the rising anger he felt swelling through his chest.

"...already everywhere you look! So what, exactly, is the problem?" Mike finished, his face flushing.

Dominique took a deep breath. He was used to Mike getting loud. As old friends, Dominique already knew Mike had always been quick to get angry and act. In tech, particularly during the mid-1990s, that had been mostly an advantage. And overall, Mike kept himself under control. As quick as he was to get amped up, Mike also generally cooled off and would admit when he was wrong. He didn't waste time looking back.

But right now, Dominique could only feel the frustration that had been building over the last six weeks, hardening into his own anger. He didn't sign up for being yelled at for doing his job well. More than that, Dominique hated that an incredible opportunity, an actual shot at making history, was turning into a half-baked, sloppy circus. One *his* reputation as the CTO of SoftAware was directly tethered to.

"Look," Dominique said. "You're right. We could technically use the AIforAll platform. It's open source, free, and easy to teach people."

"So then what—"

"There's a *lot* of problems with that," Dominique said, rising from the desk without realizing it and looking Mike in the eye. He had also raised his voice, a rare enough event that it kept Mike quiet.

"We can't guarantee our data—or anyone else's data—remains private or secure," Dominique said. "It'll be fast, sure, but the quality isn't where you think it is. And half the staff will probably panic and walk."

Mike didn't say anything, but he did scoff. Dominique took a deep breath in an attempt to control himself. He could feel the warmth creeping up into his face, and the entire core of his body felt like it was made of hot granite.

"All I'm saying is that if you give me one month, maybe three, a couple of devs, and some time, we can have our own AI that's built for what *we* do," Dominique said. "In each department. A couple of months for testing—"

"Do you think anyone else is out there *testing* this?" Mike said, his voice dangerously quiet. "This is already out in the wild. It's already being leveraged by companies that, as we speak, are using this technology to make more than we are."

Dominique could tell that, for Mike, this was a make or break moment and Mike had bought all the hype. As far as Mike was concerned, not barreling forward meant missing out. It made him even more aggravated.

"Everyone else isn't operating on three continents in 12 countries!" Dominique exclaimed, hitting the desk with his palm. "There are international regulations to consider, Mike. We're not some rinky-dink operation with the luxury of just downloading the latest app!"

Stunned at his longtime friend and business partner's reaction, Mike didn't say anything. In over two decades, Mike had never seen anything get under Dominique's skin like this.

"I'm not going to stake my professional reputation and nearly three decades in the industry on a sloppy implementation of some new tech hype cycle that we don't know anything about!"

Dominique knew he was yelling now but didn't care. He'd been excited about generative artificial intelligence and had spent many long nights devising a plan to design and deploy their own version. It would use SoftAware's data and be set up securely. It would be good for customers and the company.

Instead, this meeting Dominique had hoped would cover legal vetting processes and documentation had devolved into this shouting match. He was deeply frustrated that he and Mike could be at odds when they both wanted the same thing: to deploy generative AI.

The difference was that Dominique was not about to stake his entire professional reputation on a sloppily implemented AI initiative that didn't reflect the true potential of either his team or the tech brand he had literally helped build.

"Look, all I'm saying is let's give this a shot," Mike said, slowly sitting down to de-escalate the conversation. "You want us to build our own system, fine, I see the value in that."

Dominique exhaled and also sat down.

"OK, great," Dominique said. "So we're going to need to call legal, and I'm going to need some help to keep things running while we build this."

"Fine, fine," Mike said, waving his hand. "Just deploy the AIforAll platform at the same time."

"*Mike,* you're not listening—" Dominique said, his exasperation causing him to roll back in his chair.

"That's what you're getting," Mike said. "I want our North America and Europe customer service teams trained on this within three weeks. It can't be that different from what they're already doing."

Dominique, for the first time since he'd joined SoftAware at its founding twenty-six years ago, considered quitting.

But he saw the opportunity, too. And besides, the generic version might give some valuable information about how to engineer SoftAware's proprietary software.

"Marketing, too," Mike seied. "Make sure they're trained on using it as well."

"Sure, boss, sure," Dominique said, getting up. He knew it was all he was going to get for now, and he just hoped no huge mistakes were made in the meantime.

<u>TechEeez: Slow and Steady, But Not Winning the Race</u>

"And, there you go," Andrew said, leaning back from Kristy's desk.

Kristy, TechEeez's CFO, looked excited. Andrew felt the same way. If this went well, they could convince Lisa, the CEO, to deploy their own generative AI.

"OK, this better work," Kristy said.

"It will," Andrew said. "I'd feel better if we had more of our data in there to train it on, but I think summarizing the reports and projections will be a good start for Lisa."

Kristy was opening files and scrolling rapidly through some long spreadsheets.

"I don't get where Lisa's head is at with this," she said. "I mean, we're a *tech* company. How could we not be all over AI?"

"Yeah, I was kinda surprised, too," Andrew said, looking over Kristy's shoulder. "Maybe try an older data set first and see how it compares to your report."

Kristy nodded and opened a different file. She cut and pasted the information into the platform and typed an instruction. Within a minute, a formatted financial report summary was staring at her. Even though she'd been personally using generative AI for her own purposes—it made answering her teenager's teacher's emails *much* easier—she was still a bit shocked at how quickly responses appeared on her screen.

"Holy cow," she said. "Just *compiling* this many years worth of data would've taken me weeks. And, at least initially, it looks like the assumptions this made about sales trends in our professional soccer set actually tracks with what happened."

"Nice," Andrew said. "Give that a closer look, though and let me know what you think. If there are any issues, errors, or anything wrong that you want to see, let me know. I'm going to start building a custom version for TechEeez, or at least looking at what's available that can be customized."

"Will do," Kristy said. "Think Lisa will let you do that, though? Like, she'll pay for it? She didn't even want to let me use it for this stuff, and it's just rote reports."

"Well, she's going to have to," Andrew said. "It's happening with or without us, and I have no intention of being left behind."

"Yeah, but she thinks it's just another crypto bubble or Y2K or something," said Kristy glumly.

"I know," Andrew said. "But I figure I'll remind her how we handled the pandemic. We took all our elite training software that was deployed in professional training centers and private team gyms and adapted it to at-home use so the coaches and athletes could keep up with training."

"You did do an amazing job with that," Kristy said, remembering the press coverage. They had launched an entirely new product line and were one of the few companies tied to professional sports that had weathered the shutdown of entire stadiums rather well.

"Lisa's just scared," Andrew said. "I mean, I get it. She nearly lost everything in a crypto startup, though that company had other issues."

"I didn't know that," Kristy said. She felt her frustration with Lisa soften a bit.

"Yeah, it's why we're here now," Andrew said. "When she first came to me with the idea for this place, I could tell she wasn't that confident in it, but it also was the option she felt safest in at that point."

"So...seeing all the news coverage and everyone talking about generative AI, that's gotta bring Lisa back to a pretty bad place mentally," Kristy said thoughtfully.

"I'm pretty sure that's what's going on," Andrew said. "Don't worry, we'll get her on board."

"Well, it's up to you. I've already tried," Kristy said.

"Fear not, I'm mission ready," he joked, giving Kristy a mock salute as he left the office.

CHAPTER 3:
Results Speak for Themselves

<u>Wellness Widgets: Patience Pays Off</u>

Cheryl closed the news app on her phone and allowed herself a small, quiet smile.

The entire tech fitness space was abuzz about the imminent, spectacular downfall of another international firm. The water cooler gossip at a recent conference said the company's leadership had green lit a scattered, sloppy AI implementation. Now, the company, SoftAware, was facing multiple lawsuits in a variety of different areas and several rather serious consumer complaints. There were even whispers of a federal consumer commission investigation.

The SoftAware situation did give Cheryl—and many other leaders in this particular tech niche—pause. But whenever she read about the company's issues or gently prodded an acquaintance for details over lunch, she was consistently relieved to learn that SoftAware did everything Wellness Widgets hadn't.

Unlike Wellness Widgets, SoftAware had *yet to take* the time to develop an entirely internal AI model. From the sparse details Cheryl had gathered, SoftAware had instead relied on a patchwork of different AI platforms created by the small, overnight startups that had immediately sprouted in the wake of the first generative AI platform's deployment.

As she packed her briefcase before heading to the conference room for the all-hands meeting, Cheryl allowed herself a small sigh of relief and a small touch of pride.

It hadn't been easy for Cheryl to maintain her slower, more holistic approach over the last six months. Overnight, companies were touting their AI-based products, processes, and offerings. Particularly in the tech fitness space, for a long moment, Wellness Widgets seemed like the only company that *hadn't* released a major update to its software and products with generative AI technology.

A dizzying array of new or updated products by other fitness and wellness tech companies were released daily. There were AI-generated smoothie recipes allegedly calibrated to a person's individual fitness goals and metabolism. Every fitness app now included highly specific, tailored training plans based on a person's smartwatch data. With each passing day, the pre-AI era felt more like a distant memory despite starting only slightly over a year ago.

Everyone at Wellness Widgets felt the shift, and the excited energy in the office had begun to give way to a low undercurrent of fear.

Cheryl endured a series of tense conversations with her core team members.

Tammy, her CTO, was worried they were "missing the wave," as she put it. Before long, Tammy began to tentatively, and then more assertively, push Cheryl to launch more AI-based integrations in their existing external products. She even asked to push up release dates by four weeks, even as the Wellness Widgets employees internally testing the new AI platform reported fairly serious issues.

Cheryl managed to diffuse the tension in that conversation with Tammy using humor. She wryly reminded Tammy that the Wellness Widgets front desk receptionist, who regularly ran in charity marathons, did not have the massive heart attack the Wellness Widgets wearable had predicted.

Even Tammy smiled, remembering that incident. When the wearable's frantic beeping began to echo off the lobby's glass walls, the receptionist was sitting at her desk, calmly responding to a routine email. The receptionist had been alarmed to learn from her smartwatch that she had apparently suffered a massive coronary incident, marveling that she felt absolutely fine. It didn't take her long to realize the tech had glitched, but it was a disorienting moment all the same.

Though they'd all chuckled about the incident at the time, both Cheryl and Tammy were worried. A key feature of the integrated Wellness Widgets AI was that it would automatically call emergency services in real time if the wearable indicated the wearer was in crisis. Neither Tammy nor Cheryl wanted to deal with the false alarm fine that would have been levied if the full version of the software had been running and an ambulance had been sent. To say nothing of the embarrassment in front of the first responders. Fortunately, that feature was shut off for the testing phase.

"Our receptionist remains alive and well," Cheryl had said to Tammy with a smile. "And when a customer gets that warning in three months, we won't get sued because the customer had to pay a false alarm fine. And, we may have just saved a life."

Even Tammy couldn't argue with that.

Nevertheless, Tammy and her team spent the next few long nights fixing the issue and doing everything they could to ensure a similar event was as unlikely to occur as possible.

Unhelpfully, there were also the inevitable snags and timeline delays that came with developing a large, complex operating system and its associated software.

Then there were the non-technical items, which took time, too. In addition to the additional two to four months Tammy said were needed to create an internal Wellness Widgets LLM, the legal team's turnaround was always longer than Cheryl wanted.

Still, she made sure to have them vet any information being used to build their system for the Health Insurance Portability and Accountability Act (HIPAA), the federal legislation that protected private health data. Then, there were intellectual property concerns, an area of law that remained murky in general. In fact, Cheryl had spent so many long nights answering questions from the legal team that one of the attorneys had invited her and her husband to his wedding this spring.

Though all of these delays had been expected to some degree, each one only added to the growing tension Cheryl sensed in the office's halls. She sensed she was gradually losing some of her employees' trust, which wasn't something she could afford.

Cheryl knew that a comprehensive, responsible, secure, and robust integration and deployment of generative AI could make or break the company. She was certain she could turn it into a springboard for future growth, innovation, and success. Though she had never uttered it aloud to anyone, in the back of her mind Cheryl saw Wellness Widgets expanding internationally, perhaps even competing with SoftAware.

Adding to the pressure, Cheryl naturally was hyperaware of the significant financial investment she had made by going all in on AI integration. The spreadsheet numbers were a constant, low-level buzz in the back of her mind. There were the new developer salaries, each one a budget stretch in its own right, and then securing the additional workspace. Ensuring computational capacity was another issue with dollar signs attached to it.

Wellness Widgets was not a small company anymore, and it was in good financial health. But it also wasn't a multinational conglomerate with endless coffers or a list of VC backers, either. Cheryl had to trim expenses, leverage a few property assets that weren't being used well, and find some additional funding.

Meanwhile, Morgan, who led the customer service department, added fuel to growing company-wide concerns. Though his department remained happy with many of the internal integrations that streamlined their processes, like better shift scheduling and caller queue prioritization, there was no denying the public was clamoring for AI.

"Every call we get asks how we're integrating AI or why we don't," Morgan had said, visibly frustrated at the last meeting.

The scripts his team developed to answer those questions—written in less than an hour with the help of generative AI—explained to callers that the company would release an "advanced, fully integrated Wellness Widgets AI experience for its entire family of products and software." Though many customers were reassured and sometimes even excited, the undeniable fact was that not an insignificant number of customers had left. People associated the use of generative AI with value, and if it was lacking, in their view, so was the product.

"Don't you worry," Cheryl had told Morgan with more confidence than she felt at the moment. "Once they contact us and get to talk with a virtual representative who understands their history with us and can predict their needs better than they can, those hang-ups will all come back."

She'd ignored the surly, "They'd better," Morgan had muttered under his breath.

Adding to the challenging period was the decision to fire Joan, the marketing director. Technically, though, Cheryl had let her resign.

After all, Joan had done good work for Wellness Widgets. Her product launch campaigns and integrated advertising strategy were undeniably a significant reason for the brand's success and widespread adoption. Cheryl wanted to acknowledge that, but she also knew Joan's heart wasn't in the AI integration.

Despite giving Joan an extraordinary amount of leeway in how generative AI was deployed in her department and allowing her integrations more time to be implemented, it ultimately became clear that Joan and several members of her team were simply going through the motions.

From what Cheryl could gather, Joan and her team appeared to be paralyzed with fear when it came to integrating AI into their department and day-to-day workflow. Inevitably, it became the elephant in the room that was beginning to hold up other departments, particularly sales. Morgan's department was frustrated with the lag time in receiving marketing collaterals previewing the future generative AI versions of Wellness Widgets software. They were hoping it would assuage some of the more impatient customers.

Ultimately, Cheryl could no longer avoid the decision. Joan and her team did great work, but they had clearly shut down. Their fears and resistance to change prevented them from moving forward.

Though both women knew on an unspoken level they had been headed toward this parting of ways for a long time, it was still an awkward and tense decoupling. Cheryl knew she would miss the friendship and hoped, perhaps after some time had passed, that they could reconcile.

When Cheryl had sent a casual hello text a few weeks after Joan left, hoping the dust had settled enough, it'd gone unanswered. Though saddened, Cheryl still wished the best for Joan.

But she also worried. Unless Joan could learn to change and embrace AI as not just a technology tool or a platform but a living entity, a co-worker, and a core member of the team, Cheryl couldn't help but think Joan's career was dead in the water.

Despite all of this, on most days, Cheryl felt confident in her decision to overhaul the company inside and out to incorporate generative AI. Especially since they had been very selective about the developers they'd hired. So far, Tammy seemed happy with them and their overall work despite her impatience.

A few managers in the marketing department had left with Joan. Ever focused on the long-term outcome, Cheryl promoted a younger member of the department, Rodney, to act as the interim marketing director. Hungry and far more comfortable with the concept of digital integration overall, he immediately began integrating AI into nearly every workflow.

Within two weeks, the marketing department had a beta version of the AI platform running on everything from ad ideation to developing holistic product launches. Cheryl was seriously considering making Rodney the new marketing director, though his youth and relative leadership inexperience gave her pause. Still, she had made it a point to engage with the young man a bit more frequently than normal the past few weeks, covertly assessing his readiness for future opportunities.

All in all, it had been a long, trying, albeit exciting, few months for Cheryl. For everyone at Wellness Widgets, really.

Now, finally, Cheryl could walk into a meeting fully confident she'd made the right decision. It was already a big meeting—the last one before the full launch of a full suite of externally integrated generative AI enhancements for their entire product line. The software launch—on par with a full rebranding, really—had been a huge marketing campaign. Cheryl was pleased with how it went and the press coverage Wellness Widgets was receiving. They were one of the first larger companies in the fitness tech space to go beyond merely adopting or integrating a generative AI platform by creating and using their own version of it, nearly from the ground up.

Though Cheryl was still disappointed at how things had turned out between her and Joan, the successful unveiling of Wellness Widgets' generative AI integration reinforced her belief that she had made the right business choice. She knew Joan simply wouldn't have had the genuine enthusiasm and passion for the new, generative AI version of Wellness Widgets that the refreshed marketing team had.

What everyone else *didn't* know yet was the extraordinary news Cheryl was about to announce. She couldn't help but walk through the door smiling.

SoftAware: Crash and Burn

"What do you mean, they're 'gone'?" Mike said, his voice dangerously quiet. The only thing worse than Mike yelling was when he got "quiet angry."

"I don't know," Dominique said, running his hand over his face. He hadn't shaved—or slept, or barely eaten, for that matter—for days. Unlike Mike, however, he was practically yelling.

"I've tried emailing, calling their CEO and CTO, I even sent an email to their VC," he said. "Whatever happened, AIforAll doesn't seem to exist anymore."

Mike sat very still, numb from the deluge of catastrophic events that had transpired over the past few weeks. He looked at the papers strewn across his desk. Beneath a stack of file folders, he glimpsed a paper copy of the latest lawsuit they'd been served with.

As Mike's attorneys patiently explained that morning, SoftAware somehow did not have *permission* to run public AI software on a subcontractor's hardware. Mike had wrongly assumed this wouldn't be an issue because the hardware had been specifically built for SoftAware.

However, the subcontractor said they had yet to internally approve *any* generative AI software to run on their hardware. This was primarily because the subcontractor was scrambling to create new components that were better equipped to handle the increased computational demands of generative AI. Besides, the subcontractor's attorneys explained that the new hardware would have meant new agreements with contractors in any case.

"Had you actually discussed your own integration with us, I would have been happy to collaborate with you on this, Mike," the subcontractor's CEO had said over the phone. "As it stands now, I can't talk to you again unless our legal guys are present. Sorry, man."

With that, the line went dead.

OPPORTUNITY SEIZED, SQUANDERED, LOST: AN AI BUSINESS PARABLE

Every conversation Mike had with attorneys from that point further only enraged him. The subcontractor's attorneys explained to a furious Mike and SoftAware's legal team that the subcontractor didn't want to be liable if something went wrong, someone got hurt, or the equipment malfunctioned.

Additionally—and more importantly—the AI integration constituted a "fundamental and major change" to the previous software version. As clearly stated in the agreement, changes of that magnitude had to be negotiated and approved in writing.

SoftAware had pushed out the new, updated software that included generative AI without notifying the subcontractor, let alone asking them for technical guidance or discussing updating the licensing and contract terms.

In response, the subcontractor's attorneys issued a cease and desist letter demanding that SoftAware stop using any equipment with their hardware and cease installing any over-the-air software updates. The subcontractor rejected SoftAware's request to continue running the equipment provided they reverted the software to the previous non-AI version.

This proved to be a death knell for SoftAware. One of their core products was boutique "smart" commercial exercise machines, which comprised nearly two-thirds of SoftAware's entire commercial product line.

Hundreds of gym franchises that paid licensing fees to use SoftAware equipment—once considered premium, top-of-the-line fitness technology—were shocked to find an abrupt order to shut down all SoftAware machines in their inboxes one morning.

Many of those franchises had built their entire business model around SoftAware's trusted brand name. The franchise operators had clients download SoftAware's associated apps and fitness programs. Their gym's walls were plastered with SoftAware's logo, and the fridges behind the check-in counter sold SoftAware shakes and smoothies.

For many of the smaller gym franchises, mostly located in rural areas, the cease and desist letter was tantamount to shutting down their business, not to mention eliminating the primary income stream the franchisees needed to support their families.

SoftAware's attorneys made it clear to Mike that they were already preparing for *those* inevitable lawsuits, too.

Further legal trouble was brewing in SoftAware's European markets, where customer data was being used to train SoftAware's proprietary, in-house generative AI models. Here, too, SoftAware had failed to inform customers that their latest elliptical session, calorie logs, and run times were now training fodder for a public generative AI platform that SoftAware was currently using. This practice ran afoul of several European privacy laws.

"How could you let this happen?" Mike said, slamming his hand on the desk. "All I asked was for you to integrate software that's already out there into our systems. Didn't you think to check licenses?"

Dominique stood up, putting his hands on Mike's desk and glaring at his longtime friend and business partner.

"I'm an IT professional, not a damned lawyer," he yelled. "And in case you don't remember the hundred emails and ten phone calls, your *actual* lawyers *did* tell you this would happen. Why do you think five of them quit already?"

Dominique's face was getting red and Mike could see a vein in Dominique's neck pulse.

"None of this would be an issue if you had let me just build our own system, with *our* data and *our* guys—"

Dominique stopped abruptly.

Mike, who had never seen Dominique this angry, ever, pushed his chair back a few inches from his desk. Hot needles of panic began to prick all over Mike's body from the inside like they were trying to escape through his skin. He heard his heartbeat grow louder.

Fear was not an emotion Mike was accustomed to.

"You know what, forget this. I quit," Dominique said, suddenly talking at a normal volume. He slowly took his hands off Mike's desk and began to put his laptop back into his bag.

"What? What are you saying? You can't quit now," Mike sputtered.

"We have all this stuff to deal with," Mike said, waving at the legal documents strewn over his desk. "You need to testify and talk to the lawyers, and we need to figure out how to get the gym equipment up and run—"

"Look, I'll do whatever I'm legally required to do," Dominique said, slinging his bag over his shoulder. "And I'm going to be honest, too. I'll tell them you acted against my advice, the attorneys' advice, all of us who—"

"Wait a minute, that's not what happened," Mike interrupted, standing up. "Look, we'll do it your way from here on out, OK? We'll implement the in-house system you've been working on."

"Working on?" Dominique snorted. "When, Mike? Sure, I got a couple of guys trying to add some training data, but do you think anyone on my team has had dev time while having to babysit the cheap AI startups you've made us use? Half my guys had to teach *their* teams everything those cert jockeys don't know."

He slung his bag over his shoulder and began to walk towards the closed office door.

"Are you telling me we're not ready yet?" Mike said, suddenly angry again. "What the hell am I supposed to do? How can we keep our equipment going? And the new product accessory line—"

"That's not my problem anymore, Mike," Dominique said, turning back around towards him.

Seeing the shock on his friend's now pale face, Dominique took a deep breath and softened his tone.

"You know, there was a real opportunity here for us," he said. "I told you that at the beginning when you came back, all hyped up from that conference. And not just for you, either."

Dominique paused, hoping what he was about to say would get through to Mike, though he doubted it.

"The younger guys on my team could've been learning to be at the front edge of this tech, a way to stay relevant," Dominique continued. "It ain't always all about the bottom line, Mike. This is people's careers here. This tech is going to change the world."

"You think I don't know that?" Mike asked, enraged again. "*I'm* the one who wanted to get us in on this immediately. *I'm* the one who signs the paychecks, remember? *I'm* the one who has to stand up in that board room every quart—"

"Well, you sure haven't acted like that guy," Dominique said, moving towards the door again. "You've been acting like a jackass who only has to worry about what he wants to do with a new toy he doesn't understand."

Mike was so angry, frustrated, insulted, and hurt that he couldn't speak. He slowly became aware he was clenching both his fists.

Dominique turned around after taking a couple more steps towards the door to say one last thing. He took a long, slow look around the office. He and Mike had spent what easily amounted to thousands of hours together in this office over the past two decades. A part of him was still amazed he was leaving at all. It hadn't been a totally straightforward decision, after all. Mike was a close friend who'd spent holidays with his family. He was basically a favorite uncle to Dominique's two boys.

But Dominique knew he couldn't stay, either. And that walking out of the office meant walking out on the friendship, too.

As painful as that was, Dominique had a family to support and was too excited about working in the new tech field to let the opportunity pass him by. It was a genuine passion for technology, not profit, that had carried Dominique through the years of building SoftAware. This is what Mike didn't understand.

OPPORTUNITY SEIZED, SQUANDERED, LOST: AN AI BUSINESS PARABLE

"I was really excited, too, you know," Dominique said, his voice soft now. "I was even looking at calls for papers. I thought SoftAware would be at the front of this, *the* industry experts in AI integration."

He exhaled softly, his shoulders slumping.

"But instead, we're here," he said, glancing ruefully at the stack of legal documents on Mike's desk.

By way of a partial apology, he added, "Look, man, it comes down to this. I'm not trashing my career or this chance to be a part of history and impact on the world because of your need to be at the top of some bull *Forbes Fastest* list."

He reached the door, turning the knob, but Mike stopped him before he could leave.

"You think you get to just walk away and leave me to clean this up?" Mike hissed. "You have a contract with this company, and who do you think people will blame for these launches going to hell?"

Dominique, his hand still on the doorknob, turned and looked at Mike, his eyes now hard. "Just have your lawyers call me," he said flatly. "I'm going to be talking to them a lot either way." Without breaking eye contact, he very quietly added, "And don't you worry about me, buddy."

He took a small step back towards Mike.

"I already got offers from companies that are willing to listen to me," he said quietly. "Everyone who matters in my industry knows *exactly* how this happened, and they know damn well it's not because of me or my team. The lawyers know that, too. *My* lawyers know that, and it's real easy to prove that."

And with that, Dominique left, leaving the door to Mike's office open behind him.

TechEeez: On Life Support

Lisa consciously loosened the white-knuckle grip she had on her stylus and read the spreadsheet in front of her for at least the fifth time.

"I'm sorry, but I'm just not sure what you mean," she told Kristy, who was driving to work and on the other end of Lisa's phone. "Up until now, all the reports and projections you've been giving me were accurate. You damn near had me sold on this AI thing."

The silence coming from Lisa's Bluetooth headset was deafening, but after a minute, it finally broke.

"That's because the AI had years of data, going back to our founding, and all my prior reports to go on," Kristy said.

Although she was growing increasingly frustrated by repeating herself, Kristy tried again.

"It's like Andrew and I said when we started," Kristy said. "The AI makes inferences and predictions based on prior data and information. The more of *our* information and data it has, the better it works."

"Right, and I authorized Andrew to give you whatever you need," Lisa said, cringing at the defensiveness she heard in her voice.

"Yes, and for the quarterly reports, it was amazing," Kristy said. "Those used to take me several days, depending on the sector, and now it's done in literally minutes."

"And I appreciate that efficiency," Lisa said. "I admit getting answers to some of the more complex questions has become much faster. And yes, the expansion into the Southwest market went much more quickly and smoothly than I thought it would. Which is exactly why I gave the OK to expand this AI thing to new product projections."

Kristy audibly sighed. Lisa pushed down the anger at what was beginning to feel like impudence on Kristy's part, if not outright condescension.

"But that's different than an annual report or revenue projection," Kristy said, "especially for a totally *new* product. We've never made actual equipment or hardware before; we always stuck with the software for elite athletes and professional trainers. TechEeez's entire market is in the commercial sector, specifically professional sports team franchises."

"I'm well aware of what my own company, which I founded, makes and sells," Lisa said, her irritability seeping into her voice.

"Right," Kristy said tersely, her anger beginning to burn. "My point is that's very specific data, even within the fitness tech sector. That's why Andrew and I tried to tell you using a pre-packaged AI software bundle wasn't a good idea."

Lisa said nothing, so Kristy pushed on, her frustration causing her to grip her steering wheel tighter.

"So that means to protect our IP, we couldn't—or at least shouldn't have, Andrew is totally right about that—put all our product information and research into the AI. So, it used similar data but not *our* data. Which won't work for predictions for us because sports teams and elite professional athletes are highly specific data sets, unlike the general population sets this platform uses."

"OK," Lisa said. "But isn't the whole point of this tech that it creates instead of just synthesizes and aggregates? All I read about, every day, is all the things generative AI does on its own. Couldn't it figure out what we were asking based on the questions?"

"That's only sort of true," Kristy said, feeling a now familiar wave of anger at her boss's half-hearted attempts to keep abreast of AI and its developments.

For her part, Kristy had been attending generative AI workshops and webinars as much as she could on weekends and evenings. Even her almost daily arguments with Lisa weren't enough to dampen her enthusiasm. The more Kristy learned, the more confident she became that it could be what allowed CFOs like her to focus on more creative, effective, and efficient ways to run organizations and leverage investment capital.

Kristy had been drawn to finance because she found meeting the challenge of increasing the overall value of a company deeply fulfilling, and she enjoyed money and its mechanics on a systemic level. She saw generative AI as opening more room in her daily tasks for better, more creative analysis.

But no matter how many times she had tried to convey that to Lisa, it hadn't sunk in. Lisa seemed totally uninterested in the implications of generative AI, which baffled Kristy.

Lisa couldn't seem to get out from under the grip of her past bad experiences. And, despite Kristy's best efforts, Lisa simply couldn't grasp that generative AI would still depend on plenty of human resources to be deployed internally and externally.

Besides, if the company was planning to expand into hardware, how could it ever be successful if the new products or software *didn't* incorporate generative AI? Kristy respected Lisa as a businesswoman and company founder, which made Lisa's cognitive dissonance about generative AI all the more exasperating.

"So when the public AI platform predicted the production costs for the new hardware, that software kind of filled in the blanks on its own, based on our prior costs," Kristy went on. "But that doesn't make sense, of course, because this is a whole new level of investment for us in terms of launch timeline and product."

"Well, what were we supposed to do?" Lisa snapped. "Just hand out our IP for free to some Silicon Valley startup run by a bunch of kids?"

She was angry now. As far as Lisa was concerned, it was Kristy and Andrew's fault. All she could see now was the plans she had been carefully implementing for nearly a decade crumpling in a matter of days.

"You want us to end up like that SoftAware company, with everyone and their mother suing us?" Lisa said, outright yelling now. "This is *exactly* why I didn't want to bring any of this AI stuff in. *This* is what happens when you rely on hype cycle tech."

Kristy immediately lost her composure, unleashing her anger into her headset.

"It's *not* hype cycle tech, not if you do it right!" Kristy yelled, not even realizing she'd raised her voice.

"You're the one who wouldn't let Andrew finish our LLM, and wouldn't let me invest in a better platform," Kristy said, dismayed to find tears of anger welling up in her eyes. Even in front of another woman, there was nothing worse than crying. Kristy hated that it had gotten to this point.

"AIforAll was the only platform we could get for the measly budget we had. What did you expect would happen?" Kristy held her breath to stop the tears and forced herself to pay more attention to the road. She was approaching her freeway exit and didn't want to add a fender bender to what was already turning out to be a terrible day.

"Not to be well over sixty-five percent off the mark on projected production costs," Lisa retorted. "Not to have to put the rest of an entire new product line on hold. We may have to lay people off, you get that, don't you?"

"Well, maybe if other departments were using the AI, they could've been helping train it, too, and this wouldn't have happened," Kristy said pointedly. "Of course, *none* of this would be an issue if we just had our own system that was integrated into every department. Andrew was totally willing to—"

But it was too late. Lisa's anger had taken over, and she was forcibly jabbing at her tablet with her stylus to bring up a recent email from the head of her customer service department.

"And let's talk about the customer service issue," Lisa said, her voice quiet again but dripping with acid. "What happened there?"

Kristy cringed. She had to admit the customer service rollout hadn't turned out great. They'd used what looked like a promising AI startup, but the chatbot had begun telling customers to uninstall the TechEeez software because they—the customers—were not intelligent enough to use it. In a few other instances, the chatbots had become strangely aggressive and menacing in their tone.

"I'm not sure," Kristy said. "From what Andrew said and what I know, that platform was essentially an autocomplete type thing. I think if we'd invested in something like the avatar-based model Wellness Widgets is going to launch—"

"Oh great, your solution to broken AI is more AI," Lisa said snidely. "And I thought the whole reason we're in this mess is because you and Andrew were in such a hurry to replace people with robots. And now we've lost enough commercial clients to have to re-evaluate positions within the company. Including yours."

Kristy was silent for a long time.

Lisa rubbed her forehead. She was crushed by what the fallout of this meant. TechEeez would have to, at the very least, delay its expansion into hardware. Lisa had made decisions based on that launch and now would have to unwind some of the expansion plans, including a second office location, that were in place. Though she had never aspired to make TechEeez a huge, multi-national household brand like SoftAware, Lisa certainly understood the need to grow at least significantly at different periods.

She'd even tried to meet Andrew and Kristy partway. She made it a point to skim AI articles in the morning and realized generative AI would have to be a part of the TechEeez expansion. That's why she'd approved Kristy using it in her department and expanding into customer service.

But she wasn't going to invest a lot of capital into it, and certainly not the immense amount of time, energy, human resources, and money it would take to build an in-house generative AI model.

Which was where she and Kristy diverged.

In Lisa's view, all her careful plans were now laid to waste. She'd gone from expansion to checking to see if they could even make payroll. She was so angry, frustrated, and exhausted that she hardly knew how to plan the next phase.

As the silence grew, Lisa slowly began to calm down and realized how emotionally and unprofessionally she'd behaved. However upset she was, Lisa knew she hadn't handled the conversation well at all. A layer of shame and embarrassment lay atop her still-simmering anger. She still blamed Kristy and Andrew for this mess. In fact, she felt like Kristy was blaming *her* instead of being accountable for leading TechEeez astray.

"Look, I just pulled into the parking lot," Kristy finally said. "I'll be up in a few minutes. I need to talk to you anyway..."

Kristy paused, then decided to just say it.

"I'm leaving," she said.

Lisa, confused by the sudden shift in the conversation, furrowed her brows.

"For the day? Do you have a doctor's appointment?" she asked, forgetting that in her anger, she'd essentially threatened to fire Kristy moments before. "Actually, you're right," Lisa said. "Maybe we both should just take a day to—"

"No," Kristy interrupted. She'd shut off the car, so it was just her voice now on the line.

"I got offered a position with Wellness Widgets, and I'm taking it," she said. "They're doing some really exciting things over there with AI integration in their internal operations, and I just think it's a better fit for me."

Stunned, Lisa didn't say anything for a few beats.

"So you're going to leave, eight months away from being vested, because of a new software hype cycle?" she asked incredulously. "After all the time you've invested here with us?"

Kristy clutched her key fob tightly.

"I'll be right up," she said.

"Don't bother stopping by my office," Lisa said, her voice now hard and cold. "I accept your resignation effective immediately. You can clean out your office now and stop by HR on the way out."

With that, Lisa angrily hung up the phone.

CHAPTER 4:
To the Victor Go the Spoils

<u>Wellness Widgets: Expansion without Attrition</u>

Cheryl blinked a few times when the flashbulbs went off in front of her. She was never shy but still a bit unused to being in a room full of business reporters.

"How concerned are you about taking on SoftAware's lawsuits during this merger?" a well-known reporter asked from the audience seats. "Won't that liability negate your ability to expand into the European markets and the fitness hardware sectors?"

Cheryl smiled. She'd had to answer the same questions to the board of directors and her team several dozen times, so her response was nearly rote.

"We're expecting many of those issues to be handled quickly in arbitration or out of court," she said. "Obviously, I can't discuss details, but I can say Wellness Widgets will only use its own proprietary generative AI and cognitive AI models moving forward."

A babble of voices shouting over each other immediately began. Cheryl held up a hand until it quieted again.

"We also know that many small business owners and several subcontractors have been detrimentally impacted by some of SoftAware's decisions," she said. "Wellness Widgets looks forward to welcoming them into our ecosystem and ensuring that they are well positioned to also succeed as we make this transition."

Several more flashbulbs went off, and Cheryl saw a number of reporters frantically tapping on their phones to post her quote on social media.

"We're very excited to leverage the impressive advancements our hardware and chip manufacturing partners are bringing to the table," she said. "And we know our franchise partners and tech innovation companies share that excitement."

"How long have you been working on this?" another reporter asked, gripping her steno pad and phone recorder in one hand. "Wellness Widgets has been relatively absent on the AI scene for months; isn't this takeover a bit quick? Are you prepared for this?"

Cheryl stifled a sigh and smiled again, reminding herself that the people in the room hadn't been at her office for the past eight months.

"Quite the contrary," she said. "Everyone—and I mean everyone, including our maintenance crews and support staff—has been working on this AI integration for nearly a year. Our employees have tested and vetted every iteration of Wellness Widgets AI software."

"And our very exhausted attorneys," Tammy chimed in next to her, to a series of chuckles.

"That's how we know it's safe, reliable, and ethical AI technology," Cheryl continued. "It's also why some of SoftAware's former partners have agreed to work with us. We won't be making the same mistakes."

Next to her, Tammy fielded a few more questions about the technical aspects of Wellness Widgets AI. She was sure to mention the paper she wrote that would be published in a highly respected academic journal.

Finally, the press conference was over. Both women began the long trek across a large parking lot toward their cars together.

"I have to admit, you handled this well," Tammy said. "Did you see the email from Morgan? People are loving Ava, our avatar fitness coach. They feel like someone who knows them is answering their calls."

"I did," Cheryl said, making a mental note to stop by Morgan's office and thank him for his patience. "I do have a question for you, though."

"Yeah?" Tammy said, looking up from her phone.

"What's with that email from SoftAware's former CTO? Dom or something? I'm not clear on what he wants," Cheryl said, furrowing her brows. "Didn't he quit?"

The women had reached their cars and stopped between them to keep chatting.

"Actually, he did," Tammy said, digging through a massive handbag in search of her keys. "He wants to pick our brains about rolling out in-house AI."

"So he wants free consulting?" Cheryl asked incredulously.

"No, no, he doesn't need it," Tammy said. "Look, I know SoftAware went down in flames—luckily for us, of course—but Dominique is well-known in the industry. Every time I've talked to him at conferences, he has great ideas and knows what he's talking about. He's the real deal."

Cheryl leaned against her car's passenger door. She raised a skeptical eyebrow but didn't say anything.

"It's worth an hour meeting at least," Tammy said. "I guess he's starting his own company or something. And, to be honest, I'd love to pick *his* brain and work with him."

"Well, as long as you don't give away any secrets," Cheryl said, softening her suspicion with the joke. "Just keep me posted. I want to be on the first call, though."

Tammy grinned back.

"I don't know," she said. "It's going to be hard for you to keep an eye on us while you're on your grand tour of Europe."

"I wish there were fewer meetings and more sightseeing," Cheryl said. "As of now, my exotic adventure includes several corporate offices, a few franchise gym locations, a semiconductor plant, and a server farm."

OPPORTUNITY SEIZED, SQUANDERED, LOST: AN AI BUSINESS PARABLE

"Gee, how will you ever tear yourself away to come back?" Tammy laughed, putting her bag into her car.

"I'll just have to do my best," Cheryl laughed.

Getting into her vehicle, she had the deeply satisfying thought that she and her team *had* done their best, and that was enough to get Wellness Widgets started on the road to becoming a global brand.

Before starting her car, Cheryl took a breath and felt a moment of pride about leading the company through its AI journey. But before she had even backed out of the parking lot, she mentally began making a list of next steps, including registering for an AI webinar on ever-evolving IP laws.

Because AI was still evolving as quickly as ever. But so would Wellness Widgets. This didn't scare Cheryl. As long as they continued to treat AI like an adaptable member of the Wellness Widgets team, she knew the company's best days were ahead.

SoftAware: The Brightest Lights Burn Out the Quickest

Michael angrily scrawled his signature on the paper, barely glancing at it and slamming the pen on the clipboard.

"Have a nice day," the man in the baseball cap said, moving toward the large truck's cab. The truck was illegally parked across two handicapped spots in front of SoftAware's offices—not that it mattered. The building had been cleared out a week ago.

As the diesel engine rumbled to life, Michael was reminded of the day they had moved *into* this building: five floors, all with SoftAware's stylized logo on the doors.

Now, those doors were blank again, the offices empty. He'd stopped reading anything about SoftAware in the news, which was hard to do these days because each day brought a new story about its "AI-fueled crash." He declined all interviews with the press, which his attorneys had told him to do in any case.

Mostly, Mike spent his time bitterly wondering when taking the lead in innovation had become so difficult. As far as he was concerned, SoftAware's downfall wasn't due to his recklessness and impatience but rather red tape and legal machinations that served little to no purpose.

Still, Michael knew this was a setback. OK, he'd let his enthusiasm get the best of him. He should have been more careful in implementing AI and listened to his team more. Mike laid the blame for the company's failure squarely on Dominique's shoulders. If he had gotten behind Mike, if he could have only seen the vision instead of throwing up roadblocks and constantly arguing, Mike was certain SoftAware would have catapulted to new heights.

Mike had made no effort to reach out to Dominique. The men communicated solely through lawyers. For a brief second, Mike had considered sending Dominique's son the college graduation gift he'd bought the young man a month earlier. Instead, he threw the gift away. These days, he didn't think about Dominique or his family unless he had to for legal purposes. That was the past, and Mike never spent time on the past.

The friendship may be over, but Mike wasn't convinced this was the end of SoftAware.

Once the lawsuits were behind him—and several of them looked ready to settle, though the slog through the legal system was painfully slow—he could start a different venture. He still had some capital and a few assets he could leverage. After all, that moving truck was moving his personal office furniture to a storage unit.

Agreeing to the Wellness Widgets sale had deeply hurt his pride. Mike had dismissed the growing company as a serious competitor only a few months before when his marketing team brought them up in a meeting. Well, if they wanted this mess, they could have it. Mike didn't think their CEO was equipped to handle a global enterprise anyway.

Despite SoftAware's failure, Michael remained certain he was still the right person to lead the way into a future propelled by generative AI. He walked towards his car, a sleek Alpha Romeo he'd bought to celebrate SoftAware's entry into the EU market.

He made a mental note to purchase his plane ticket to Nairobi. The AI workers there had voted to unionize, but Mike wasn't too worried about that. Workers were easy enough to appease, and when compliance couldn't be bought cheaply enough, it could always be coerced.

SoftAware was not Mike's first company and was one of only a handful of failures. Overall, he had been successful in the tech space, so some of the larger global tech conglomerates still valued his insights into ways to leverage generative AI.

Mike preferred being a CEO to a consultant, but until the dust settled, this would do for now. He certainly had plenty of lessons to share.

TechEeez: Treading Water

Lisa sighed as she packed up her bag after what seemed like a very long day. Actually, it felt like the last six months had been one long day.

Walking down the empty, dark hallway to the elevator, she felt another pang of regret. TechEeez, she reflected as she looked at the company logo by the elevator button, was still standing.

But that was more of a bittersweet thought than a comforting one. While she had been working towards a small, but not insignificant, expansion of the TechEeez product line, none of that was feasible now.

Instead, Lisa had leveraged everything she could to pay her new AI integration consultant, Dominique. She'd been leery about hiring him, especially since he came from SoftAware, but they'd enjoyed a good working relationship so far. He was clearly knowledgeable and personable besides.

One thing that changed was that Lisa listened to Dominique's guidance and implemented his advice with very little pushback. She knew when to admit she was wrong and was determined not to make the same mistake twice.

She had to lay off some staff to hire Dominique's firm, and the idea of a second office location was now at least two years away. But, importantly, it was not impossible.

Dominique seemed certain that once TechEeez launched its new software platform, the company could gain some footing again. Thanks to its rather specific market, he seemed certain TechEeez could still position itself to be competitive with similar-sized companies.

After all, TechEeez did have several decades of brand trust and recognition. The scuttled product launch wasn't public. For many of the sports teams, aspiring Olympiads, and elite athletes who still used TechEeez software and devices, the company just seemed slower to adopt AI. Lisa was grateful for that, at least.

OPPORTUNITY SEIZED, SQUANDERED, LOST: AN AI BUSINESS PARABLE

With Andrew, her CTO, gone, Lisa needed some good tech council. The past few months had been painfully humbling for her. It felt like the crypto crash all over again. After all, she had been a phreaker in high school. She wasn't used to being the person behind the curve when it came to innovation, especially in her own field.

Lisa sighed a bit as the elevator doors opened to the empty car garage. Her heels echoed against the concrete pillars. She hoped the online panel discussing new AI legislation that evening wasn't too complicated so she could cook dinner while listening to it. It seemed all she did anymore was play catch-up on AI developments, news, and events.

But she *would* make time for the webinar. If one thing were true for Lisa and TechEeez moving forward, it would be that she would be far more aware of how tech innovations could impact employees personally. And she would never dismiss disruptive technology or trends as a hype cycle so easily again.

Further Thoughts to Consider

Thoughts on AI Large Language Models (LLMs)

Today's LLMs being utilized within AI deployments at their core, are based on statistics, linear algebra, and math involving large scale matrices. Remember the adage, "There are lies, damn lies, and statistics?" This holds true especially with AI. To reduce error in statistical modeling, enough quality (scrubbed and validated) data needs to be fed into the model to reduce "error" (what the AI sector calls "hallucinations"). Hallucinations and biased outputs from an LLM are nothing more than a "less correct" answer based on the data available to analyze against the question (or task) being requested of the LLM by the user.

AI is Personal—it's about the Human and the Business

Recently I was at a conference, listening to a panel discuss AI when an audience member asked a question. "I am an author," he said, "and I uploaded some of my writing to the AI and asked it to learn about my writing style." He went on to describe how he then asked the LLM to complete a half-finished novel "in his voice." Imagine his surprise when the LLM deviated from his "voice" and proceeded to complete the novel by "pulling feminist language" into his writing style.

After the talk, I engaged the author to better understand his challenge. I asked him how many stories he uploaded to train the model? His response was that he uploaded three "long" stories and few "short" stories. His lack of general awareness around this action highlighted the "personal" or human concern that we see in many businesses testing and evaluating AI today and is one of the reasons we illustrated this situation within the TechEeez team's AI journey as the "reporting disaster" highlighted in the story. Another example is Mike and his team at SoftAware rushing headlong into using an AI platform and tool, without fully understanding which tool is best to drive a specific business outcome. This approach created significant internal tension, confusion, and frustration within leadership and employee ranks, and it was disastrous not just for the business, but for all stakeholders including customers, partners, employees, and owners.

Because the author I was speaking to failed to plan, educate himself, and develop the skills required to utilize the AI platform and tool in a safe and risk-managed manner, he has put himself and his intellectual property at risk. When I suggested that now, because of the licensing agreement he failed to read thoroughly (and just scrolled through), all of his uploaded/trained data was now included in the LLM (and was no longer truly protected from theft as he had not registered any copyrights for his work) he began to realize the personal and professional result of his actions and became pale.

This oversight is no different than the amateur golfer buying the most expensive set of clubs, thinking that tools make up for a lack of knowledge, preparation, and skill. **<u>In short, tools enhance people and skills, they do not replace them</u>**...The author I chatted with had done the same thing. He had not considered that getting the LLM to "write like him" would require massive amounts of his own works, significantly more than he had ever written (and would likely ever write). And, in uploading the (small) amount of work he had completed, he now exposed that work for the LLM to leverage.

Enabling an LLM to impact business, financial, employee, and customer processes and decisions inside of your organization, without considering the human impact, and providing enough clean and validated data for the LLM, is a recipe for disaster.

There's a Difference Between the Tortoise, Hare, and Sloth

Aesop's fable of the race between the tortoise and the hare was made for childhood learning for millennia. As well, the core story of patience and persistence winning the race, is fundamentally aligned in our story between Mike and Cheryl, the hare and tortoise, respectively. However, we realized that Aesop should have considered a third animal to introduce in his fables—that of the sloth. The sloth moving SO SLOWLY as to never truly engage in the race. Lisa and TechEeez exemplify the concept of the sloth. The slothful business never moves forward (or moves so slowly as to not appear to be moving) to what might be a new business opportunity, thereby losing any/all benefit.

Consider the Ripples Made by the Rock Thrown

The very different approaches taken by Mike and Cheryl around implementing AI into their business highlights the ripple effect leadership decisions can make. Our core recommendation is to consider the personal impact that AI will have on employees, partners, and customers. This approach can be the difference between creating significant business value through an AI deployment and experiencing value destruction. Almost daily, employees globally are consuming fear-based marketing messages that AI is going to replace their jobs. Consider how Cheryl approaches the AI topic with her team—acknowledging that AI is personal, addressing her team's concerns with empathy, layered with pragmatism. She realizes that automation, and efficiencies in process can create the potential of SOME activity and employee redundancy, so she needs to take that into consideration as she navigates her AI journey. Keeping the number of negatively impacted employees to a minimum should be a consideration and goal for any leadership team. This will require leadership teams to revisit their organizational design, the core competencies within their organization, and will require both leadership teams and employees to master change management, as they develop new skills, capabilities, and "retool."

Your upstream and downstream partners might not be as aligned as you are—they might lean more like Mike than Cheryl. Or worse, they are like Lisa and might cause significant delays in value creation simply because they are not "on board" with how to leverage AI. Just as impactful as moving too slow, some partners might try to force you to accelerate your own implementation of AI to meet their needs. Do not fall into the trap of being a supply chain lemming. As a business leader, you need to closely examine your partnership value chain and openly query your peers on how they are implementing AI. If their perspective, approach, and core values do not align with yours, consider recommending this book to them. Another option might be to leverage this opportunity to examine value chain alignment and develop partnerships with others that align to your core values and goals around AI.

OPPORTUNITY SEIZED, SQUANDERED, LOST: AN AI BUSINESS PARABLE

In the movie "Star Wars: Episode IV, A New Hope" (yes, we are both geeks at heart), there is a scene where one of the protagonists—Princess Leia—declares to the movie's "big boss"—Grand Moff Tarkin, "The more you tighten your grip, Governor Tarkin, the more star systems will slip through your fingers." This declaration has alignment to how your customers may react to any EXTERNAL implementation of AI. For example, assumptions that clients will gladly engage with a chatbot instead of a person are often met with poor customer satisfaction, churn, and revenue erosion. Purposefully pushing customers into automated "self-service" functions (or leveraging the latest video/text/audio mashup of "AI customer service reps") is a sure way to drive clients into the arms of a competitor that offers a more personalized and warmer "human" customer experience. This is especially true in business-to-business value chains, where the interactions are often more complex, and dollars per transaction are (often) significantly higher than business-to-consumer markets. In other words, be purposeful in your approach to external AI uses. Don't attempt to squeeze your customers into AI workflows without appropriate testing, change management, and listening enabled.

Living Within Your Means

No organization looking to leverage AI has unlimited resources and funds. Those companies building AI models right now, or supplying the technologies to enable AI, are the darlings of the market and are experiencing nine, ten, or even higher double-digit valuation growth. For example, at the time of this edition, nVidia is the market darling having just reported 262% year-over-year revenue growth for the quarter. The businesses looking to leverage these technologies can only hope to have the type of valuation growth nVidia has seen. Limited access to resources and funds means that careful planning and pragmatic expectations must be set by you and your leadership team. Thoughtful cash management and appropriate value creation goals and milestones can lead to positive business outcomes such as accelerated revenue and profit growth, and the increase in corporate valuation. Tapping the capital markets to secure investments that will accelerate AI implementation within your business might appear to be a solid decision. However, the ownership dilution that comes with that approach may prove challenging versus implementing some short-term cost controls offset by the eventual revenue growth. In other words, is the juice from taking on capital partner(s) worth the squeeze provided through dilution of your ownership? It may be worth it, especially if you have recently been engaged in a leadership role of a "sloth-like" business like TechEeez. But unintended costs to ownership and potential downstream exit strategies could occur as a result.

Onboarding AI like a Human

There is a personal development, organizational design, and leadership development concept that leverages an arborist best practice—"trimming to grow better". We recommend that as you begin your AI journey, that you onboard AI as if it is a living entity, a human, an employee. This will cause you to evaluate the organization, your business model, strategy, organization, employees, and day-to-day operations, and identify areas that need trimming and cultivating. If you onboard AI technologies as you would an employee, you will educate and train the AI tools on your vision, mission, customers, employees, partners, KPIs, metrics, operating procedures, etc. Onboarding AI in this manner will cause you to define specific business goals, objectives, plans, and outcomes that you wish to achieve through the application of AI within your business. Through this process your leadership team and employees will identify areas within the business that can be AI powered or enabled. In turn, those activities should lead to the creation of AI use cases and a list of initiatives or internal pilots that the team will begin to test. AI becomes your internal corporate arborist, helping leadership and employees to identify areas of the business to trim and cultivate for the corporate to not just survive, but thrive and grow stronger. Through this approach, AI becomes more human, a valued member of the team, and will be more engaged and adopted inside the culture and team.

We would welcome your thoughts, questions, and feedback on this book, the stories within, and the approaches we discussed. Please reach out to us at connect@s3ntrycorp.com. We look forward to hearing from you.

THE END

Don't miss out!

Visit the website below and you can sign up to receive emails whenever Mark Dallmeier and Edward Vasko publishes a new book. There's no charge and no obligation.

https://books2read.com/r/B-A-PZRRB-PXNID

BOOKS2READ

Connecting independent readers to independent writers.